D0463895

York, 1991

Medieval
Gardens
A BOOK OF DAYS

Medieval Gardens

A BOOK OF DAYS

Poems selected by
KEVIN CROSSLEY-HOLLAND

O Paradise! thy rival is this place ...

English 12th century. Bishop Hildebert de Laverdin: De Ornatu
Mundi

GARAMOND

First published in Great Britain in 1990
by Garamond Publishers Ltd
Strode House, 44-50 Osnaburgh Street,
London NW1 3ND

Designed by Tim Scott

Printed and bound in Italy

ISBN 1 85583 031 0

Illustrations
Front cover: *Early season labour*
Back cover and half-title: *The common garden*
Title: *Enjoying the late evening*

Prologue

He who would a gardener be
In this book can hear and see
Every day of the month and year
And what skills he must master.

English. 15th century. John Gardener: The Feate of Gardening

January

_____ 1

_____ 2

_____ 3

_____ 4

_____ 5

_____ 6

_____ 7

A secret tryst

This January, so noble, and so old,
Found walking in it such felicity
That no one was allowed to have the key
Except himself, and for its little wicket
He had a silver latch-key to unclick it
Or lock it up, and when his thought was set
Upon the need to pay his wife her debt
In summer season, thither would he go
With May his wife when there was none to know,
And anything they had not done in bed
There in the garden was performed instead.

English. 14th century. Geoffrey Chaucer. : The Canterbury Tales

January

_____

_____ 8

_____

_____ 9

_____

_____ 10

_____

_____ 11

_____

_____ 12

_____

_____ 13

_____

_____ 14

_____

January

15

16

17

18

19

20

21

A declaration of love

Around the coping of these wells
And beside streams, above all else,
The grass sprang up, so soft, thickset,
Quite as fine as any velvet,
On which a man his love could lay
As on a featherbed, to play.

English. 14th century. Geoffrey Chaucer: Romaunt of the Rose.

January

	22
	23
	24
	25
	26
	27
	28

Early planting

l

If you want roses in winter, pick little buds from the rose bush, with long stems, and put them in a small wooden barrel, such as a compost barrel, without any water. Have the barrel sealed and bound so that it is completely watertight, and tie a large and heavy stone to each end of the barrel, and lay the barrel in a running stream.

French. 1393. Le Menagier de Paris. *Anonymous*

January

_____

29

_____

30

_____

31

_____

Winter games

Tending the lawn

Get a garden! What kind you may get matters not,
Though the soil be light, friable, sandy and hot,
Or alternatively heavy and rich with stiff clay;
Let it lie on a hill, or slope gently away
To the level, or sink in an overgrown dell –
Don't despair, it will serve to grow vegetables well!

Latin. 9th century. Walafrid -Strabo: *Hortulus (De Cultura Hortorum).*

February

1

2

3

4

5

6

7

$\mathfrak{I}$ leave the whole plot to be baked, like a bun,
By the breath of the south-wind and heat of the sun.
Only, lest the soil slip and drift out of its place,
With four pieces of timber I edge the whole space,
And then heap the bed up on a gentle incline.
Next, I rake till the surface is powdered and fine;
And lastly, to make its fertility sure,
I impose a thick mulch of well-rotted manure.
And now – a few vegetable seeds let us sow,
And watch how the older perennials grow!

Latin (Swabia). 9th century. Walafrid Strabo: Hortulus (De Cultura Hortorum)

February

8

9

10

11

12

13

14

February

15

16

17

18

19

20

21

Courting couple

Rose

Gardeners say that rosemary seeds never germinate in French soil; but whosoever picks branches of rosemary and strips them of leaves from top to bottom and plants them in the earth will see them grow. And if you want to send branches such as this any distance, wrap them in waxed cloth and sew up the cloth, smear the outside of the parcel with honey, then powder it with wheat flour, and you can send the branches wheresoever you like.

French. 1393. Le Menagier de Paris. *Anonymous*

February

22

23

24

25

26

27

28/9

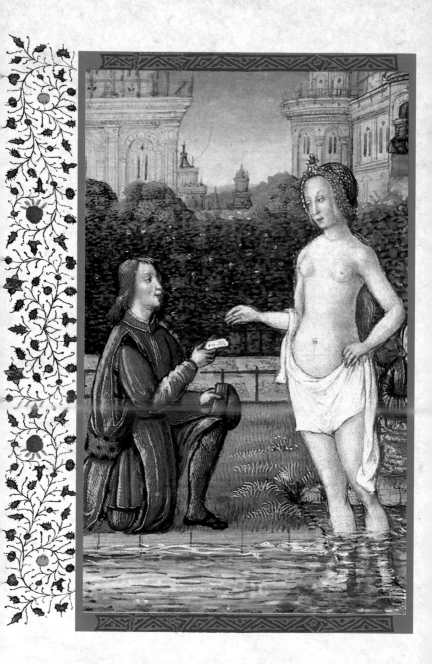

March

1

2

3

4

5

6

7

A letter arrives

We wish the villa owner to have gardens in which to exercise by walking, or for banquets as the occasion demands. The gardens will have exotic plants and excellent little trees, very artfully and properly arranged. In them topiary work in myrtle, box, citrus, and rosemary is most highly to be recommended. For the raison d'être of gardens should not be the same for the splendid man as for the thrifty and gain-seeking father of a family. The gardens contribute wonderfully to the splendour of the villa, which is not rustic but a magnificent villa urbana.

Italian. 16th century. Giovanni Pontano

March

_____

8

_____

9

_____

10

_____

11

_____

12

_____

13

_____

14

_____

March

15

16

17

18

19

20

21

Early window boxes

A garden teems with ants, but if you throw sawdust
from oak planks on to their hill, the ants will die or leave
when rain next falls, because the sawdust retains the
moisture.

French. 1393. Le Menagier de Paris. Anonymous

March

22

23

24

25

26

27

28

March

29

30

31

Spring planting

April

_____ 1

_____ 2

_____ 3

_____ 4

_____ 5

_____ 6

_____ 7

_____

Enjoying the first fruit

$\mathfrak{I}$t behoves the man who would prepare the site for a pleasure garden, first to clear it well from the roots of weeds, which can scarcely be done unless the roots are first dug out and the site levelled, and the whole well flooded with boiling water so that the fragments of roots and seeds remaining in the earth may not by any means sprout forth. Then the whole plot is to be covered with rich turf of flourishing grass, the turves beaten down with broad wooden mallets and the plants of grass trodden into the ground until they cannot be seen or scarcely anything of them perceived. For then little by little they may spring forth closely and cover the surface like a green cloth...Upon the lawn too, against the heat of the sun, trees should be planted or vines trained, so that the lawn may have a delightful and cooling shade, sheltered by their leaves.

German. 13th century. Albertus Magnus: De Vegetabilibus et plantis

April

_____

8

_____

9

_____

10

_____

11

_____

12

_____

13

_____

14

_____

April

15

16

17

18

19

20

21

Spring courting

April

22

23

24

25

26

27

28

April

29

30

Entertainment in the open air

Lazing on a Spring day

Green turf amid silent trees and soft light airs
And a spring of running water in the grass,
They freshen a jaded mind, they give me back to myself,
They make me abide in myself.

Latin (France). 12th century. Marbod of Rennes: Meditation among Trees

May

_____

1
_____

2
_____

3
_____

4
_____

5
_____

6
_____

7
_____

It was the morning of the sixth of May
And May had painted with her softest showers
A gardenful of leafiness and flowers;
The hand of man with such a cunning craft
Had decked this garden out in pleach and graft,
There never was a garden of such price
Unless indeed it were in Paradise.
The scent of flowers and the freshening sight
Would surely have made any heart feel light
That ever was born, save under the duress
Of sickness or a very deep distress;
Pleasure and beauty met in every glance.

English. 14th century. Geoffrey Chaucer: The Canterbury Tales

May

_____

8

_____

9

_____

10

_____

11

_____

12

_____

13

_____

14

_____

May

15

16

17

18

19

20

21

First fruit of Summer

I turned to wander at mine ease
Beneath the burgeoning mulberry trees,
Laurels, lithe hazels, and dark pines,
Throughout the garden's far confines.

French. 13th century. Guillaume de Lorris and Jean de Meung:
Roman de la Rose

May

22

23

24

25

26

27

28

May

29

30

31

Outdoor love

June

_____ 1

_____ 2

_____ 3

_____ 4

_____ 5

_____ 6

_____ 7

Two lovers hiding under a fennel tree

Behind the abbey, and within the wall of the cloister, there is a wide level ground: here there is an orchard, with a great many different fruit-trees, quite like a small wood. It is close to the infirmary, and is very comforting to the brothers, providing a wide promenade for those who want to walk, and a pleasant resting-place for those who prefer to rest. Where the orchard leaves off, the garden begins, divided into several beds, or still better cut up by little canals... The water fulfils the double purpose of nourishing the fish and watering the vegetables.

French. 12th century. Anonymous

June

8

9

10

11

12

13

14

June

15

16

17

18

19

20

21

Gathering daisies

And in the garden, as the sun rose,
She walked up and down wherever she chose.
She gathered flowers, some white, some red,
To make a subtle garland for her head,
And she sang with the voice of an angel.

English. 14th century. Geoffrey Chaucer: The Canterbury Tales

June

22

23

24

25

26

27

28

June

29

30

Following pages: *My lady's garden of treasure*

Eastern delight

July

_____ 1

_____ 2

_____ 3

_____ 4

_____ 5

_____ 6

_____ 7

Landscaping for the Lord of the Manor

Bees do not perch on fruit but on fresh flowers, and from them they gather the substance from which they make both honey and wax. And when the flowers near the hive are spent, they send spies to search for meat further afield. If night falls while they're on the wing, these spies lie upright so as to protect their wings from rain and from dew, so that they can fly to work all the more quickly in the morning, on dry wings. Bees keep night watch as men do in castles, and rest all night until day dawns, when one bee rouses all the others by buzzing two or three times, or making some other loud noise. Then they all fly out of the hive, if it is a fine morning.

English. Bartholomaeus Anglicus: de Proprietatibus Rerum

July

_____

8

_____

9

_____

10

_____

11

_____

12

_____

13

_____

14

_____

July

15

16

17

18

19

20 .

21

Garden of angels

b ſcrio tr domi
na ſancta mari
a mater dei pie
tate pleniſſima

July

22

23

24

25

26

27

28

July

29

30

31

Full bloom under a blue sky

Garden of inspiration

August

_____ 1

_____ 2

_____ 3

_____ 4

_____ 5

_____ 6

_____ 7

Go into the garden at dawn on Sunday and on bare knees say three Ave Marias and three Paternosters in reverence to the Trinity, then take a cabbage or some other leaf eaten by caterpillars and put inside two or three of them, and say 'Caterpillars come with me to Mass'; then take the whole thing along to church, and before listening to the Mass let it fall. After this the caterpillars will disappear from the garden – this is not a joke, it has been proved to work and its practice is still in use.

Italian. 16th century. Girolamo Firenzuola

August

_____ 8

_____ 9

_____ 10

_____ 11

_____ 12

_____ 13

_____ 14

_____

August

15

16

17

18

19

20

21

Proposing in the Garden of Love

Fruct uidracum

August

22

23

24

25

26

27

28

August

29

30

31

Making music

September

_____ 1

_____ 2

_____ 3

_____ 4

_____ 5

_____ 6

_____ 7

_____

Unicorn in the Garden of Myth

Then in we went to the garden glorious,
Like to a place of pleasure most solacious.

With Flora painted and wrought curiously,
In divers knots of marvellous greatness;
Ramping lions stood up wonderously,
Made all of herbs with dulcet sweetness,
With many dragons of marvellous likeness,
Of divers flowers made full craftily,
By Flora coloured with colours sundry.

Amidst the garden so much delectable
There was an arbour fair and quadrant,
To paradise right well comparable,
Set all about with flowers fragrant;
And in the middle there was resplendent
A dulcet spring and marvellous fountain,
Of gold and azure made all certain.

·

English. 1509. Stephen Hawes: The History of Grand Amour and la Bell
Pucell

September

8

9

10

11

12

13

14

September

15

16

17

18

19

20

21

Tending the garden

I am a winter fruit that has less tenderness
Than summer fruit, so I am kept in store
To soften my too green hardness,
Set to ripen in the straw of prison.

French. 15th century. Charles d'Orleans: Ballade LXXX

September

22

23

24

25

26

27

28

September

_____

29

_____

30

_____

Contented couple

October

1

2

3

4

5

6

7

Forester at work

And she arose and clad her in a goodly gown that she had of cloth-of-silk; and she took bedclothes and towels, and tied one to other and made a rope as long as she could, and made it fast to the window-shaft; and so got down into the garden. Then she took her dress in one hand before, and in the other behind, and girded herself, because of the dew she saw heavy on the grass, and went her way down the garden... Her little breasts swelled beneath her clothes like two nuts of a walnut-tree. And her waist was so fine that your two hands could have girded her; and the daisy-flowers snapped by her toes, and lying on the arch of her foot, were fairly black beside her feet and ankles, so very white the girl was.

Picardian French. 13th century. Aucassin et Nicolette. *Anonymous*

October

8

9

10

11

12

13

14

October

15

16

17

18

19

20

21

A pleasant outdoor afternoon

October

22

23

24

25

26

27

28

October

29

30

31

Round the garden there was no wall or fence except of
air; yet by magic the garden was enclosed on every side by
air so that nothing could enter it, any more than if it were
ringed about by iron, unless it flew in over the top. And
all summer and winter it had flowers and ripe fruit. Now
the nature of the fruit was such that it could be eaten
inside, but to take it out was impossible; for if anyone did
want to carry any out, he would never get back to the gate
or ever leave the garden until he had put the fruit back in
its place.

French. 12th century. Chrétien de Troyes: Erec et Enide

November

_____

1

_____

2

_____

3

_____

4

_____

5

_____

6

_____

7

_____

The first harvest

If possible a clear fountain of water in a stone basin should be in the midst, for its purity gives much pleasure. Let the garden stand open to the North and East, since those winds bring health and cleanliness; to the opposite winds of the South and West it should be closed, on account of their turbulence bringing dirt and disease; for although the North wind may delay the fruit, yet it maintains the spirit and protects health. It is then delight rather than fruit that is looked for in the pleasure garden.

German. 13th century. Albertus Magnus: De Vegetabilibus et plantis

November

8

9

10

11

12

13

14

November

15

16

17

18

19

20

21

A stroll in the meadow

To find a pearl, or a precious stone, or a farthing, or something similar, inside an apple: after it has flowered and begun to swell, take an apple and thrust in one of the aforesaid objects at the bud-end; then allow it to grow, and make a careful note of which apple you put the thing into, whatever it was!

English. 15th century. Anonymous

November

22

23

24

25

26

27

28

November

_____

29

_____

30

_____

A picnic feast

December

1

2

3

4

5

6

7

My lady's gardener

A gardener should have a fork, a wide blade, a spade or shovel, a knife...a seed-basket for seed-time, a wheel-barrow (more often a little hand-cart), basket, pannier and trap for sparrow-hawks...a two-edged axe to uproot thorns, brambles, briars, prickles and unwanted shoots, and rushes and wood to mend hedges...timbers, palings, and stakes or hedging hurdles...he should also have a knife hanging from his belt to graft trees and seedlings, mattocks with which to uproot nettles or vetch, darnel, thistles, sterile oats and weeds of this sort, and a hoe for tares.

English. 12th century. Alexander Neckham: De Utensilibus

December

8

9

10

11

12

13

14

December

15

16

17

18

19

20

21

Preparing the patch

In a glorious garden green
Saw I sitting a comely queen
Among the flowers that fresh been.

She gathered a flower and sat between.
The lily-white rose me thought I saw,
The lily-white rose me thought I saw,
And ever she sang.

English. 16th century. The lily-white rose. *Anonymous*

December

22

23

24

25

26

27

28

December

29

30

31

Drinking from the fountain

Epilogue

Now withers the rose, and the lily is spent,
And both once bore the sweetest scent,
In summer, that sweet time.

English. 13th century. Anonymous

Outdoor games

Picture Credits

Picture Credits

November 1:   British Library, London, Ms. Add 19720, fol. 6/104 16.
November 22:   Bibliothèque Nationale, Paris, Ms. 6021, fol. 231v.
December 22:   British Library, London, Ms. 3781, fol. 1.

Borders
January: Bibliothèque Nationale, Paris, Ms. Fr. 807, fol. 346.
February   Bibliothèque Nationale, Paris, Ms. 23278, fol. 122.
March: Bodleian Library, Oxford, Ms. 488.
April   Bibliothèque Nationale, Paris, Ms. 1156B, fol. 163.
May: British Library, London, Ms. Roy 14E VI, f. 208
June: Walters Art Gallery, Baltimore, Ms. 274 f. 8v.
July   Bibliothèque Nationale, Paris, Ms. 1173, f. 2v.
August   Bibliothèque Nationale, Paris, Ms. Fr. 242, fo. 17.
September   Bibliothèque Nationale, Paris, Ms. Fr. 616, fo. 27v.
October: British Museum, London, Ms. 1069, f. 1.
November: The Ellesmere Manuscript, Shuckburgh Reynolds (Ph: Bridgeman).
December   Bibliothèque Nationale, Paris, Ms. 247, f. 25.